How Artists See PLAY

Sports Games Toys Imagination

Colleen Carroll

ABBEVILLE KIDS

A DIVISION OF ABBEVILLE PUBLISHING GROUP

New York London

"Painters understand nature and love her and teach us to see her."

—VINCENT VAN GOGH

For Charlie and Arlene, with love.

I'd like to thank the many people who helped make this book happen, especially my editor, Jackie Decter; Ed Decter; Colleen Mohyde; Patricia Fabricant; Jennifer O'Connor; Scott Hall; Jo-Anne Faruolo; and, as always, my husband, Mitch Semel.

—COLLEEN CARROLL

JACKET AND COVER FRONT: Jacob Lawrence, *Munich Olympic Games,* 1971 (see also pp. 10–11). JACKET AND COVER BACK, LEFT: Maxfield Parrish, *The Reluctant Dragon,* 1900–1 (see also pp. 28–29); RIGHT: Jean-Baptiste-Siméon Chardin, *Soap Bubbles,* c. 1733–34 (see also pp. 20–21). JACKET BACK, BOTTOM: Dick West, *Cheyenne Winter Games,* 1951 (see also pp. 16–17).

EDITOR: Jacqueline Decter
DESIGNER: Jennifer O'Connor
PRODUCTION EDITOR: Meredith Wolf Schizer
PRODUCTION MANAGER: Lou Bilka

 The text of this book was set in Stempel Schneidler. Printed and bound in China.

First library edition
10 9 8 7 6

ISBN-13: 978-0-7892-0393-9
ISBN-10: 0-7892-0393-6

Library of Congress Cataloging-in-Publication Data
Carroll, Colleen.
Play : sports, games, toys, imagination / Colleen Carroll. 1st library ed.
p. cm. — (How artists see, ISSN 1083-821X)
Includes bibliographical references .
Summary: Examines how sports, games, toys, and other aspects of play have been depicted in works of art from different time periods and places.
ISBN 0-7892-0393-6
1. Play in art—Juvenile literature. 2. Visual perception—Juvenile literature. [1. Play in art. 2. Art appreciation.] I. Title. II. Series: Carroll, Colleen. How artists see.
N8236.P47C37 1999
704.9'4979—dc21 98-46412

For bulk and premium sales and for text adoption procedures, write to Customer Service Manager, Abbeville Press, 137 Varick Street, New York, NY 10013, or call 1-800-ARTBOOK.

Visit Abbeville Press online at www.abbeville.com.

CONTENTS

THE RACES AT LONGCHAMP

Edouard Manet

All people know what fun it is to play. Just think for a moment what your life would be like if you couldn't throw a ball with your best friend, play with your favorite toys, or let your imagination take you on all sorts of fantastic adventures. Without play, the world would be a pretty dull place. Because playing is so important to people and so much fun, it's a subject that has always been a favorite of artists, from ancient times right up to today. Now keep reading to discover how artists see play, and perhaps you'll recognize some of the special ways you like to play.

And they're off! On this beautiful day at the races the artist shows you the action from the middle of the track. How does this dramatic viewpoint help you sense the speed and excitement of the race? The artist put the paint on the canvas with loose, free strokes of his brush to give the scene a blurry look, as if you were glimpsing the race only for a split second. Pretend you are a jockey on one of these horses. How do you think it would feel to be in this race? What would it sound like to you?

ASTRA
ELAUNAY
YORK-PARIS-

THE CARDIFF TEAM

Robert Delaunay

In this picture of a rugby match, one player leaps into the air to make the catch. He's surrounded by his opponents, and it's nearly certain that in the next few moments he'll be tackled to the ground. Do you think he'll be able to hold on to the ball? Why do you think the artist chose to show this particular moment?

As the player reaches for the ball, your eye is drawn upward into a sky filled with amazing things. The artist used simple shapes and vivid colors to create activity in the sky that is just as exciting as the action on the playing field. What things do you recognize?

DISKOBOLOS (THE DISCUS THROWER)

Myron

This sculpture was made in Greece over two thousand years ago. Just like people today, the ancient Greeks believed that everyone should be physically fit. The artist carved his sculpture to capture the athlete's strength, determination, and grace. What details show you these qualities?

The athlete is just about to hurl the heavy disk through the air. It takes strong muscles and balance to do this. Put yourself in this position, spin around three times, and let go of an imaginary discus. Which muscles did you use?

Jacob Lawrence

MUNICH OLYMPIC GAMES

Jacob Lawrence

One of the oldest and most popular sports is running. In this picture of an Olympic relay race, the artist captures the moment just before one of the athletes crosses the finish line to victory. By using bright colors and strong curving lines, the artist makes it seem that the runners are flying toward the white tape with lightning speed and boundless energy. To feel the action of the race, put your finger at the top of the track and move it around the curve toward the finish line with a fast sweeping motion. Who do you think will win?

NOFRETARI PLAYING DRAUGHTS

Egyptian

People love to play games, all sorts of games. Games can be silly, like peekaboo; challenging, like chess; or suspenseful, like hide-and-seek. In this ancient wall painting a queen is happily playing draughts—a game similar to checkers—without an opponent. Why do you think the artist showed the queen playing draughts by herself?

She sits in a room decorated with many hieroglyphic symbols, the picture language of the ancient Egyptians. Some of the symbols will look familiar to you. What do you think the symbols mean?

Even though the queen's body looks stiff, her elegant robe seems to flow gracefully to the floor. By giving the robe many gently curving lines, the artist creates a feeling of movement in an otherwise static picture. Trace your finger along the lines of the queen's dress to experience the course of the artist's brush.

二葉草七小町
清水小町
哥麿筆

BLINDMAN'S BUFF

Kitagawa Utamaro

The object of this game, called Blindman's Buff, is for the person who is "it" to find the other players—blindfolded! Here the boy who is "it" leans back on one leg and holds his hands up in front of his body. Why do you think he is standing in such an awkward position? His sister stands a safe distance away. Where do you think she should hide?

As you just saw in *Nofretari Playing Draughts,* the artist who made this woodblock print used lines in clever ways. He placed the children's mother behind a sturdy screen made of many horizontal and vertical lines. The screen remains still, while the mother's flowing kimono seems to cascade to the ground. She holds part of her robe over her mouth to suppress a giggle. What do you think she is feeling as she watches her children play?

CHEYENNE WINTER GAMES

Dick West

In this lively picture, a community of Native Americans are enjoying a winter field day. How many different events do you see? You probably can find some games that you've played before; others may look unfamiliar to you. Point to some of the games you know. If you could jump into the picture, which game would you like to play?

In their buckskin clothing the people stand out sharply against the white snow. You can see that the people who seem closest to you are also the biggest, while those who seem farther away are smaller. The artist composed the picture in this way to create an illusion of distance and space. Look for the people who are placed far into the background. What are they doing? Does this scene seem lively and fun? Why?

MARBLES CHAMPION

Norman Rockwell

There's a saying that goes like this: every picture tells a story. This particular story is about three children playing a game of marbles, and much, much more. You can figure out a lot about the characters in this story just by looking at their faces. Each child has a very different expression. Which child is winning? How can you tell? If you were to write this story, how would it end?

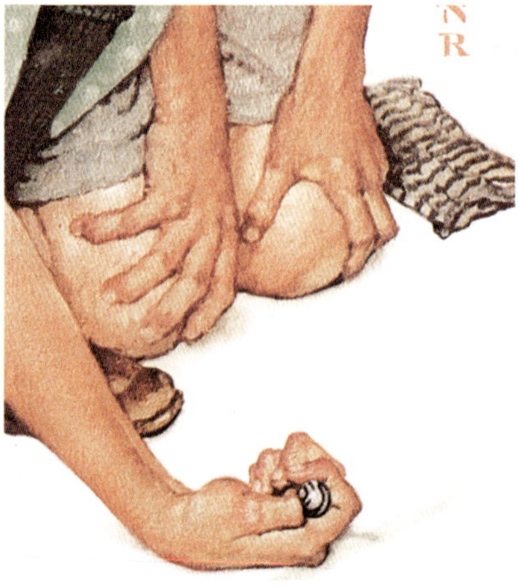

The artist brings his "story" to life with many interesting details, such as the fabrics of the children's clothing and the empty bag once full of marbles. What other details do you see?

SOAP BUBBLES

Jean-Baptiste-Siméon Chardin

Everybody has a favorite toy. Even grown-ups like toys. Toys can be fancy or simple, such as the one in this picture. Take a straw and a glass of liquid soap, and you have all the ingredients you need for hours of wondrous play. If you've ever blown bubbles, you know just how magical it can be. As the boy in this picture blows a bubble through a slender straw, his face is full of patience and concentration. What words would you use to describe the other boy's expression? The bubble is growing quite large. How much bigger do you think it will get before it bursts?

The artist painted this picture in a very true-to-life style. It's as if you could almost pick up the glass of soap, rest your elbow on the stone ledge, and even pop the bubble with your finger. To give the picture this realistic quality, the artist included many lifelike details, such as the cracks in the stone surface. Point to some of the other realistic details.

CHILDREN PLAYING ON THE BEACH

Mary Cassatt

No day at the beach would be complete without a pail and shovel. Here you see two young girls happily digging in the sand. What do you think each is doing? Imagine

yourself on this sunny stretch of beach. What would you build with a pail and shovel?

This painting has a very natural feeling, as if you were walking along the beach and happened to come upon these two little girls playing with their toys. If you were to stroll past them at the exact moment that you see in the picture, do you think they would notice you?

Mary Cassatt

THE CIRCUS

Alexander Calder

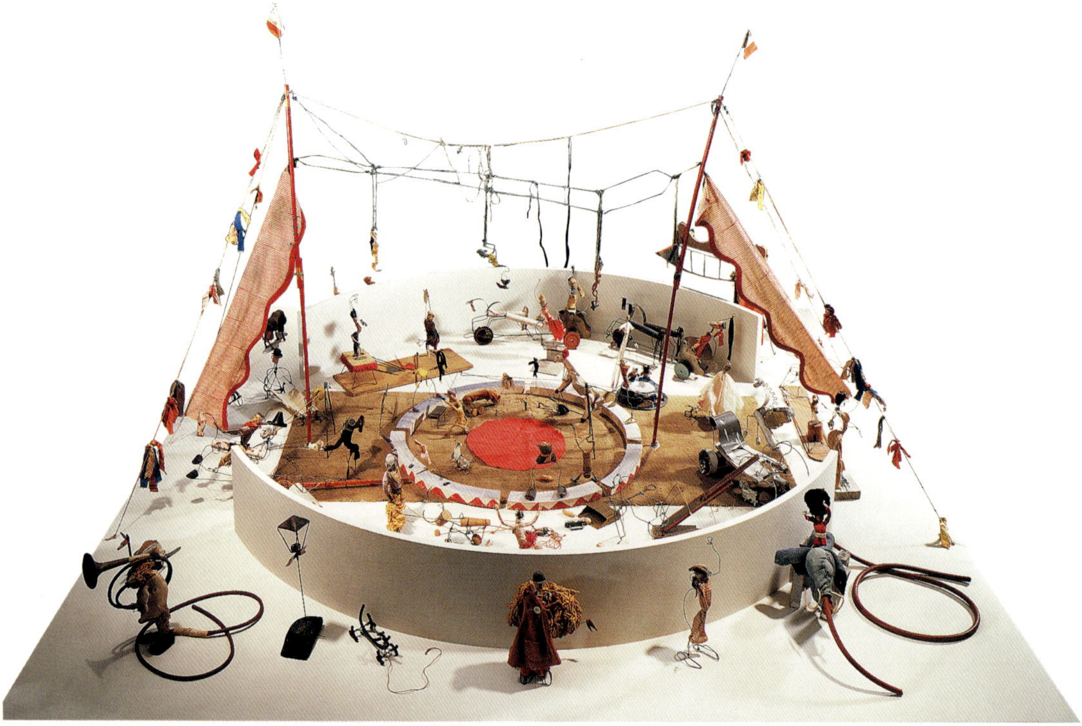

Step inside the big top and witness a most unique scene: a miniature toy circus! Which circus acts and performers do you recognize? Pretend you are just a few inches tall and a member of this unusual troupe. In which act would you be the star?

The artist who made this sculpture loved to make toys, such as the buckaroo you see below. He created his entire circus out of ordinary wire and a variety of other materials. What are some of the other materials he used?

TOYS

ANNETTE'S DOLLS

Jonathan Green

In this picture a little girl named Annette poses on a flowered sofa with her treasures. Can you find her among her dolls? It's clear that Annette likes to collect dolls and stuffed animals. Perhaps you have a collection of your own. If not, what do you think would be fun to collect?

The artist who made this painting likes to use bright colors and bold patterns. Even though there is no movement in the picture, the different patterns placed around and next to each other make the scene lively and fun to look at. How many different patterns can you spot?

THE RELUCTANT DRAGON

Maxfield Parrish

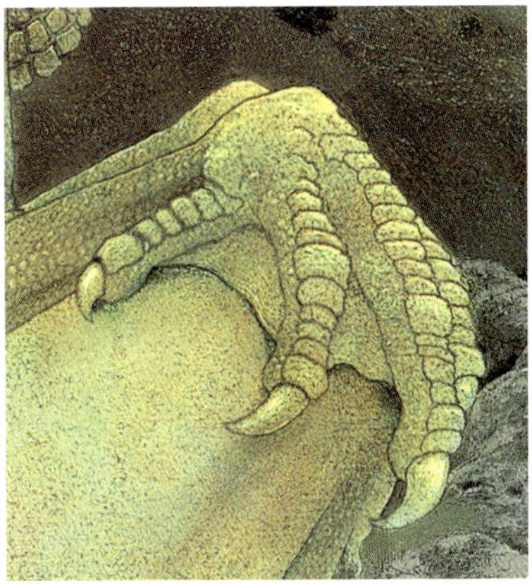

Using your imagination, you can go anywhere you want to go, even to faraway lands where dragons live. Here a young boy and a dragon sit quietly on a stony hill, staring at each other. Look at the expressions on their faces. What do you think each is thinking about the other? The title of this picture is *The Reluctant Dragon.* The word *reluctant* means to be unwilling or hesitant. Why do you think this dragon is reluctant?

Since everyone knows that dragons don't really exist, the artist had to use his imagination to create one that looks, well, real. Although it's a fantastical creature, the artist based his dragon on a combination of many different kinds of animals. Look carefully at the dragon's body. What animals do you think the artist was imagining when he painted this whimsical dragon?

PAULO AS PIERROT

Pablo Picasso

Playing dress-up, putting on costumes, and pretending to be someone or something else can be a whole lot of fun. Here you see the artist's son Paulo dressed as Pierrot, a well-known character from the French theater. In his floppy white costume, Paulo stands against a plain black background and patch of light blue sky. The only decoration the artist included are the fancy iron bars of the balcony. Why do you think he chose such a simple setting for this portrait?

Paulo strikes a playful pose: hands on hips and ready for any comical situation to occur. Why do you think the artist chose to paint his son with his mask off? Now look at his face. Does he look like he's having fun? What might he be thinking? Pretend you are going to have your portrait painted while in costume. What kind of costume would you wear?

THE MAGIC FLUTE

Marc Chagall

If you could paint a picture of your dreams, what would it look like? In this picture, the artist has created a dreamscape of his own imagination. In a magical forest, an angel hovers in the air, playing a tune on a flute. All around the angel are creatures that seem to float, free from the gravity that would normally hold them to the earth. Perhaps it is the beauty of the angel's music that makes them soar. What does the melody sound like to you?

The artist used just four colors in his picture. Two are cool colors—the blue and green. They help to give the picture a feeling of tranquillity. The other two, red and yellow, are warm colors. What mood or feeling do they give to the picture?

THE NEW NOVEL

Winslow Homer

Nothing sparks the imagination like a good book: reading takes your mind on all sorts of adventures and journeys.

In this watercolor painting, a young girl is engrossed in her new novel. Her eyes are fixed on the pages as she reads. If you could tiptoe into the picture, do you think she'd hear you approaching? She could be reading a mystery, a romance, a thriller, or a fantasy, to name but a few. What types of books fire your imagination?

As you have just seen, artists have many ways of showing people at play. Go back to the beginning and look at all the pictures again. Which ones appealed to you the most? Did any of the subjects remind you of how you like to play? Now think about your favorite sports, games, and toys, or use your imagination and create your own artwork about the world of play in your own personal style.

NOTE TO PARENTS AND TEACHERS

As an elementary school teacher I had the opportunity to show my students many examples of great art. I was always amazed by their enthusiastic responses to the colors, shapes, subjects, and fascinating stories of the artists' lives. It wasn't uncommon for us to spend an entire class period looking at and talking about just one work of art. By asking challenging questions, I prompted the children to examine and think very carefully about the art, and then quite naturally they would begin to ask all sorts of interesting questions of their own. These experiences inspired me to write this book and the other volumes in the *How Artists See* series.

How Artists See is designed to teach children about the world by looking at art, and about art by looking at the world through the eyes of great artists. The books encourage children to look critically, answer—and ask—thought-provoking questions, and form an appreciation and understanding of an artist's vision. Each book is devoted to a single subject so that children can see how different artists have approached and treated the same theme, and begin to understand the importance of individual style.

Because I believe that children learn most successfully in an atmosphere of exploration and discovery, I've included questions that encourage them to formulate ideas and responses for themselves. And because people's reactions to art are based on their own personal aesthetic, most of the questions are open-ended and have more than one answer. If you're reading aloud to your children or students, give them ample time to look at each work and form their own opinions; it certainly is not necessary to read the whole book in one sitting. Like a good book or movie, art can be enjoyed over and over again, each time with the possibility of revealing something that wasn't seen before.

You may notice that dates and other historical information are not included in the main text. I purposely omitted this information in order to focus on the art and those aspects of the world it illustrates. For children who want to learn more about the artists whose works appear in the book, short biographies are provided at the end, along with suggestions for further reading and a list of museums where you can see additional works by each artist.

After reading *How Artists See Play,* children can do a wide variety of related activities to extend and reinforce all that they've learned. In addition to the simple activities I've suggested throughout the main text, they can design and create a toy or board game, put on a play, or organize a neighborhood field day that includes their favorite sports. Since the examples shown here are just a tiny fraction of the great works of art that feature play as their subject, children can go on a scavenger hunt through museums and the many art books in your local library to find other images of play.

I hope that you and your children or students will enjoy reading and rereading this book and, by looking at many styles of art, discover how artists share with us their unique ways of seeing and depicting our world.

ARTISTS' BIOGRAPHIES

(in order of appearance)

If you'd like to know more about the artists in this book, here's some information to get you started:

EDOUARD MANET (1832–1883), *pp. 4–5*

Manet (pronounced *ma-NAY*) believed that artists must "be of their own time and work with what they see," and paint in new and bold ways. Many people didn't agree with him. Some of his paintings made people very angry because of just how new they looked. This French artist put his paint on in thick, free strokes of the brush that made his subjects look flat. Most people who saw his work weren't used to this new style, but a small group of painters learned many lessons from Manet that they used in their own painting. These young painters came to be known as the Impressionists (look back at *Children Playing on the Beach*), and Manet as the "father of Impressionism."

ROBERT DELAUNAY (1885–1941), *pp. 6–7*

In the early twentieth century the city of Paris was a hotbed of many different styles of art. The artist Pablo Picasso (look back at *Paulo as Pierrot*) was busy creating an entirely original style of painting called Cubism, in which the subject seems to be broken into pieces and put back together again at many different angles. The French painter Robert Delaunay (pronounced *deh-loe-NAY*) began his career as a painter at age eighteen. Several years later he began painting Cubist pictures, but in his own unique style, using bright colors and overlapping shapes that made his paintings look like stained-glass windows. He called this style Orphism, which means "orchestra of color." He liked to experiment with color and movement, and he was also interested in machines, especially the mechanical inventions of the day, such as airplanes. He liked to paint many pictures of the same subject, and his series of paintings of the Eiffel Tower is one of his most famous. His dynamic and colorful style influenced the work of many artists of the twentieth century, including Marc Chagall (look back at *The Magic Flute*).

MYRON (WORKED C. 480–450 B.C.), *pp. 8–9*

In the nearly 600-year span of the Ancient Greek civilization, the arts were greatly valued and artists were highly respected people. The Greeks, who were the inventors of democracy, believed in the integrity of the individual, or the goodness of each and every human being. One of the civilization's most important writers, Sophocles, said, "Wonders are there many—none more wonderful than man." In the fifth century B.C., known as the Classical period, artists created a new style of sculpture that celebrated the beauty and spirit of man in a way that had never been done before. Earlier sculptures of people appeared stiff and motionless, but Classical artists made sculptures that look natural and seemed to express feelings and movement. These sculptors paid great attention to detail, such as clothing and hair styles, and that made their subjects look even more lifelike. One of the most skilled sculptors of this period was Myron, an expert at making sculptures in bronze. Although none of his original works exist today, many Roman copies clearly show how gifted an artist he was. His *Diskobolos* is one of the most famous sculptures of all time.

JACOB LAWRENCE (BORN 1917), *pp. 10–11*

"My paintings express my life and experience." The artist who spoke those words, Jacob Lawrence, was born in Atlantic City, New Jersey, and later moved with his family to Pennsylvania. After his parents separated, Lawrence and his siblings were first placed in foster homes but were eventually reunited with their mother in the Harlem section of New York City. Shortly thereafter he enrolled in an after-school art class and decided to become a painter. In 1940 he began his masterpiece series, The Migration of the Negro. Its sixty painted panels and text written by the artist told the epic story of the great migration (1916–30) of African Americans, including his parents, who left the rural South to work in the northern industrial centers of the United States. This series made Lawrence an "overnight success." Lawrence's artwork is noted for its simple, flat shapes, bold colors, and social themes. After teaching art for many years at the University of Washington, Jacob Lawrence retired in 1983. He still lives and makes art in Seattle.

ANCIENT EGYPTIAN PAINTING (NEW KINGDOM, 1500–1162 B.C.), *pp. 12–13*

Pyramids, sphinxes, and great stone temples are just some of the wonders of Ancient Egypt, a civilization that flourished for more than two thousand years and produced some of history's most amazing works of art. Although the ancient Egyptians are best known for their sculpture and architecture, wall painting was also an important part of Egyptian art. Paintings were used to decorate the walls of temples and tombs. In combination with hieroglyphics (the system of pictures and symbols that make up the Egyptian language), scenes were painted in bold colors and with figures heavily outlined in black. The paintings often depicted stories from the lives of gods, goddesses, kings, and queens. Ordinary people, too, had tombs decorated with wall paintings, and it is from these pictures that historians learn about the way the people of this great civilization lived.

KITAGAWA UTAMARO (1753–1806), *pp. 14–15*

Even when Kitagawa Utamaro (pronounced *oo-tuh-MAH-roe*) was a young man being trained by a master painter and printmaker, he showed great talent and individuality of style. He received his training in the Japanese style known as ukiyo-e. *Ukiyo-e,* which was popular from 1603 to 1867, means "the floating world," and the artists who worked in this style depicted happiness and the pleasures of daily life. When Utamaro was thirty-five he published an album of prints called *The Insect Book,* which brought him widespread acclaim and popularity, but he is best known for his woodblock prints of beautiful women and famous actors of the Japanese theater. His art and that of other ukiyo-e artists influenced the French Impressionists and the American painter and printmaker Mary Cassatt (look back at *Children Playing on the Beach*).

DICK WEST (1912–1996), *pp. 16–17*

"My early training was very peculiarly Cheyenne . . . according to tradition. And this I gained from my grandparents and I feel—I've always felt—that I had to portray a true authentic thing [the history and culture of the Cheyenne people]." In the Cheyenne language the Native American artist Dr. Walter Richard West is called Wah-Pah-Nah-Wah, which means Light Foot Runner. West was orphaned as a youngster, and he and his brothers grew up with their grandparents in Oklahoma. He studied fine arts at Bacone College, a school in Oklahoma for Native Americans, and received his graduate degree from the University of Oklahoma. He is known for his drawing skills, his fine use of line and color, and his great attention to detail. If West didn't know how something should look he would ask the older members of his tribe for information and then research his subject in the library. He won many prestigious awards and was a strong influence on the many students he taught during his long lifetime.

NORMAN ROCKWELL (1894–1978), *pp. 18–19*

If every picture tells a story, then American illustrator Norman Rockwell told hundreds of them during his career. Illustrators are artists who make pictures for books, magazines, and newspapers. Because so many people were able to see his paintings and drawings on the covers of popular magazines, his work became very well known. People looked forward to his sweet and funny scenes of everyday life—children playing, people working, and family holidays. Rockwell often asked friends and neighbors to model for him, and this lively cast of characters shows up again and again in his pictures.

JEAN-BAPTISTE-SIMÉON CHARDIN (1699–1779), *pp. 20–21*

As a painter living in France during the eighteenth century, Jean-Baptiste-Siméon Chardin (pronounced *shar-DAN*) was unique. Instead of painting decorative pictures of rich people in fancy clothes or busy pictures of mythological stories like most artists of that time, Chardin painted simple still lifes, which show objects arranged together in a pleasing way, or pictures of people doing everyday things, such as playing cards or returning home from a day at the market. These kinds of pictures are known as genre scenes. Chardin's style was very natural and realistic, and he had a remarkable ability to capture the many qualities of light. Because other artists made engravings of his paintings and printed them in large numbers, he became quite well known during his lifetime.

MARY CASSATT (1844–1926), *pp. 22–23*

Born into a wealthy family, the American painter Mary Cassatt (pronounced *kuh-SAHT*) traveled throughout Europe when she was young. On these trips she was exposed to the works of the European masters and decided to become a professional artist. She studied art at the Pennsylvania Academy of Fine Arts in Philadelphia and later in Italy and Paris, where she moved in 1874. There she met the Impressionist artist Edgar Degas. They quickly became friends and soon Cassatt began painting in a style similar to Degas's and the other Impressionists', and she even exhibited her own work with them on many occasions. She is best known for her portraits of mothers with their children and of women doing everyday activities, such as sealing a letter or adjusting a veil. Besides being an accomplished painter, she was also a printmaker, and many of her prints were influenced by the Japanese woodcuts so popular in late-nineteenth-century Paris (see *Blindman's Buff*).

ALEXANDER CALDER (1898–1976), *pp. 24–25*

The son and grandson of sculptors, this American artist learned from an early age how to make things. As a young man living in Paris, France, he made his now famous wire *Circus,* complete with movable clowns, animals, and acrobats. He is best known for his mobiles—sculptures made of flat, metal shapes that look like objects from nature, such as fish, leaves, and animals. These sculptures hang from the ceiling on heavy wire and move with the changing air currents. Calder also made large metal sculptures known as stabiles (like the word *stable*). These stabiles, which don't move, are most often found in wide, open spaces, such as city squares and sculpture gardens. In 1998 there was a major exhibition of the work of this beloved twentieth-century artist at the National Gallery of Art in Washington, D.C.

JONATHAN GREEN (BORN 1955), *pp. 26–27*

"I know I can't save a whole culture, but as an artist I can help create greater awareness, perhaps." These words, spoken by the American painter Jonathan Green, refer to the culture of the Sea Islands, a predominantly African-American community off the coast of South Carolina. Green honed his artistic skills at the school of The Art Institute of Chicago, a very prestigious school for serious young art students, but it is his memories of growing up on the South Carolina Sea Islands that inspire his work. His paintings capture a proud people carrying out the traditions and rituals of their daily lives, such as worshiping in church, casting fishing nets into the water, braiding hair, and hanging crisp, white sheets on a clothesline. Each of his paintings is a celebration of life. Green is the recipient of many honors and awards, including a 1996 honorary doctorate in fine arts from the University of South Carolina and the Martin Luther King, Jr., Humanitarian Award for the Arts. He lives and works in Florida, and in addition to painting has illustrated two popular children's books (see Suggestions for Further Reading).

MAXFIELD PARRISH (1870–1966), *pp. 28–29*

Frederick Parrish was born into an artistic family. His father, a painter, taught him to draw and paint while he was recovering from a serious illness. The family took trips to Europe, and Fred became fascinated with the medieval towns and villages he saw there. This fascination showed up in his later artwork in the form of dragons, castles, kings, and courts. After the family's second trip to Europe, young Fred Parrish decided to become an artist. First he studied architecture, but after three years he switched to art school. It was around this time that he began calling himself Maxfield—the last name of his maternal grandmother. By the age of twenty-five he was working as an illustrator, and his pictures appeared in many national magazines. He also began illustrating popular children's books; his first book of illustrations was a volume of *Mother Goose* rhymes. To create his pictures, he would dress models in costumes and photograph them in a variety of poses. Then he would cut out the photos, arrange them in a pleasing composition, and paint the pictures based on that arrangement. He didn't like to mix his colors and often painted directly from tubes of vividly colored paint. He lived most of his adult life as a member of an artists' colony in Vermont, and his one-word-title pictures are among the most recognizable of the twentieth century.

PABLO PICASSO (1881–1973), *pp. 30–31*

Picasso (pronounced *pea-KAH-so*) was born in Spain, but for most of his life he lived and painted in France. Many people consider him the most important artist of the twentieth century. Picasso began to draw as a young boy, and after attending art school he moved to France, where he would help change the course of art. Throughout his long life he explored many different styles of art, but he is perhaps best known for a style called Cubism, in which the subject seems to be broken into many shapes and is seen from many angles at once. Picasso lived to be an old man, and his many paintings, drawings, sculptures, and ceramics can be seen in museums all over the world.

MARC CHAGALL (1887–1985), *pp. 32–33*

This popular artist was born into a large, poor Russian family that taught him to love and appreciate the traditions of Jewish life. As a boy he attended art schools in St. Petersburg, a large city in Russia, and then moved to Paris to pursue his career as an artist. He chose the right time to be in Paris, which was the center the art world in the early part of the twentieth century. Chagall quickly became known worldwide as a gifted painter of brightly colored fantasies that combine memories of childhood with the experiences of living in a vibrant, modern city. This versatile and gifted artist also created stained-glass windows, theater sets and costumes, prints, drawings, and ceramics. His works have been widely reproduced, and that has helped to make him one of the world's most well-known and beloved artists.

WINSLOW HOMER (1836–1910), *pp. 34–35*

The American artist Winslow Homer was born in New England but moved to New York City as a young man to become an illustrator. When the Civil War broke out, Homer was hired by a popular magazine to paint pictures of the front. After the war he continued making illustrations but spent more and more time painting scenes from everyday life in the realistic style he is famous for. In 1881 he traveled to England, where he lived in a seaside fishing village, an experience that took his art in a new direction. When he returned to America he began to paint—in both watercolors and oils—rugged pictures of the sea. He liked to use watercolor paints to sketch scenes from nature, especially the seaside, and he used some of these watercolor studies as ideas for his oil paintings. Winslow Homer is one of America's most beloved artists because he was able to capture the spirit and beauty of a young nation in his art.

SUGGESTIONS FOR FURTHER READING

The following children's titles are excellent sources for learning more about the artists presented in this book.

FOR EARLY READERS (AGES 4–7)

Sellier, Marie. *Chagall from A to Z.* Translated from the French by Claudia Zoe Bedrick. New York: Peter Bedrick Books, 1996.
In this charming and beautifully illustrated book, the letters of the alphabet introduce elements of the Russian painter's long life and career.

Venezia, Mike. *Picasso.* Getting to Know the World's Greatest Artists series. Chicago: Children's Press, 1988.
This easy-to-read biography combines color reproductions and humorous illustrations to capture the personality and talent of the famous twentieth-century artist.

FOR INTERMEDIATE READERS (AGES 8–10)

Gauch, Patricia Lee, and Jonathan Green. *Noah.* New York: Philomel Books, 1994.
With illustrations inspired by memories of his Sea Islands childhood, artist Jonathan Green helps create a charming and unique rendition of the classic Bible story.

Howard, Nancy Shroyer. *Jacob Lawrence: American Scenes, American Struggles.* Worcester, Mass.: Davis Publications, 1996.
Engaging text, colorful illustrations, and fun activity ideas combine to give a thorough introduction to the life and art of Jacob Lawrence.

Lawrence, Jacob. *The Great Migration: An American Story.* New York: Harpercrest, 1993.
In his own words and pictures, the American artist tells the story of the thousands of African Americans who left the South in search of work and a better life in the industrial North.

Weatherill, Sue, and Stephen Weatherill. *Hieroglyph It: Discover the Picture Language of the Ancient Egyptians.* New York: Barron's, 1995.
This activity package contains materials for children to experiment with Egyptian hieroglyphics, including project ideas and booklet, stencils, papyruslike paper, and a symbol chart.

FOR ADVANCED READERS (AGES 11+)

Beneduce, Ann Keay. *A Weekend with Winslow Homer.* New York: Rizzoli, 1993.
This informative and clever book takes the reader back in time to meet the American painter, who narrates the story of his life and work.

Burrell, Roy, and Peter Connolly. *Oxford First Ancient History.* Rebuilding the Past series. New York: Oxford University Press, 1994.
History comes to life on this factual and engaging journey through the ancient

world, including the civilizations of Egypt, China, Greece, and Rome.

Lipman, Jean, and Margaret Aspinwall. *Alexander Calder and His Magic Mobiles.* New York: Hudson Hills Press, 1981. In this colorful and interesting book, the authors introduce readers to more than forty works by the American sculptor. The engaging text reviews Calder's life and career, often using the artist's own words.

Meadows, Matthew. *Pablo Picasso.* Art for Young People series. New York: Sterling Publishing Company, 1996. The author takes the reader on a voyage through the life and career of the twentieth century's most famous artist with a survey of Picasso's many styles, periods, and accomplishments.

WHERE TO SEE THE ARTISTS' WORK

ALEXANDER CALDER

- Fort Wayne Museum of Art, Indiana
- Freeport Art Museum and Cultural Center, Illinois
- Hirshhorn Museum and Sculpture Garden, Smithsonian Institution, Washington, D.C.
- Moderna Museet, Stockholm
- Museum of Fine Arts, Springfield, Massachusetts
- National Gallery of Art, Washington, D.C.
- Neue Nationalgalerie, Berlin
- Oklahoma City Art Museum
- Stamford Museum and Nature Center/Leonhardt Galleries, Connecticut
- University of Rochester Art Gallery, New York
- Whitney Museum of American Art, New York
- Haggerty Museum of Art, Marquette University, Milwaukee, Wisconsin
- McNay Art Museum, San Antonio, Texas
- Masur Museum of Art, Monroe, Louisiana
- Metropolitan Opera House, Lincoln Center, New York
- Museum of Modern Art, New York
- Nassau County Museum of Fine Art, Roslyn Harbor, New York
- Stedelijk Museum, Amsterdam
- Sunrise Art Museum/Fine Art Museum, Charleston, West Virginia
- The Union Church, Pocantico Hills, New York

MARY CASSATT

- The Art Institute of Chicago
- Cleveland Museum of Art
- Dallas Museum of Art
- The Metropolitan Museum of Art, New York
- Musée d'Orsay, Paris
- National Gallery of Art, Washington, D.C.
- Nelson-Atkins Museum of Art, Kansas City
- Philadelphia Museum of Art
- Pushkin Museum of Art, Moscow
- http://watt.emf.net/wm/net

MARC CHAGALL

- The Art Institute of Chicago
- Solomon R. Guggenheim Museum, New York

JEAN-BAPTISTE-SIMÉON CHARDIN

- The Art Institute of Chicago
- Ashmolean Museum, Oxford
- Louvre Museum, Paris
- The Metropolitan Museum of Art, New York
- Museum of Fine Arts, Springfield, Massachusetts
- National Gallery, London
- National Gallery of Art, Washington, D.C.
- Allen Memorial Art Museum, Oberlin College, Ohio

ROBERT DELAUNAY

- The Art Institute of Chicago
- Solomon R. Guggenheim Museum, New York
- Kunstmuseum, Basel
- Musée d'Art Moderne de la Ville de Paris
- Museum of Modern Art, New York
- Philadelphia Museum of Art

ANCIENT EGYPTIAN TOMB PAINTING

- British Museum, London
- Brooklyn Museum of Art
- Egyptian Museum, Cairo
- Louvre Museum, Paris
- The Metropolitan Museum of Art, New York
- Museum of Fine Arts, Boston
- Oriental Institute, Chicago

JONATHAN GREEN

- Afro-American Cultural Center, Charlotte, North Carolina
- Afro-American Museum of Philadelphia
- Beach Institute Museum Collection, Savannah, Georgia
- Gibbes Museum of Art, Charleston, South Carolina
- Greenville County Museum of Art, Greenville, South Carolina
- IFCC Cultural Center Portland, Oregon
- McKissick Museum, Columbia, South Carolina
- Morris Museum, Augusta, Georgia
- Norton Gallery Museum, West Palm Beach, Florida
- Philharmonic Center for the Arts, Naples, Florida

WINSLOW HOMER

- Addison Gallery of Art, Phillips Academy, Andover, Massachusetts
- Amon Carter Museum, Fort Worth
- Arizona State University Art Museum, Tempe
- Delaware Art Museum, Wilmington
- Freer Gallery of Art, Smithsonian Institution, Washington, D.C.
- Museum of Fine Arts, Springfield, Massachusetts
- National Museum of American Art, Smithsonian Institution, Washington, D.C.
- North Carolina Museum of Art, Raleigh
- Pennsylvania Academy of the Fine Arts, Philadelphia
- Portland Museum of Art, Maine
- Wichita Art Museum, Kansas

JACOB LAWRENCE

- Bellevue Art Museum, Washington
- High Museum of Art, Atlanta
- Museum of Modern Art, New York
- National Academy of Design, New York
- National Museum of American Art, Smithsonian Institution, Washington, D.C.
- The Phillips Collection, Washington, D.C.
- Seattle Art Museum
- Studio Museum of Harlem, New York
- Frederick R. Weisman Art Museum, University of Minnesota, Minneapolis
- http://hudson.acad.umn.edu/Lawrence/WAMjacobtest.html

EDOUARD MANET

- The Art Institute of Chicago
- The Barnes Foundation, Merion, Pennsylvania
- Courtauld Institute Galleries, London
- Charles and Emma Frye Art Museum, Seattle
- Fogg Art Museum, Cambridge, Massachusetts
- John Paul Getty Museum, Los Angeles
- Heckscher Museum, Huntington, New York
- The Metropolitan Museum of Art, New York
- Musée d'Orsay, Paris
- National Gallery, London
- Norton Simon Museum of Art, Pasadena, California

MYRON AND CLASSICAL GREEK SCULPTURE

- Acropolis Museum, Athens
- Archeological Museum, Olympia
- The British Museum, London
- John Paul Getty Museum, Los Angeles
- Louvre Museum, Paris
- Museo Nazionale Romano delle Terme, Rome
- The Metropolitan Museum of Art, New York
- Staatliche Antikensammlungen und Glyptothek, Munich

MAXFIELD PARRISH

- American Illustrators Gallery, New York
- Anschutz Collection, Denver
- Charles Hosmer Morse Museum of Art, Winter Park, Florida
- Mask and Wig Clubhouse, Philadelphia
- Museum of Fine Arts, Boston
- National Academy of Design, New York
- New Britain Museum of American Art, New Britain Connecticut
- Redferne Gallery, London
- St. Regis Hotel, New York

PABLO PICASSO

- Albright-Knox Art Galley, Buffalo
- Arkansas Art Center, Little Rock
- Art Gallery of Ontario, Toronto
- The Art Institute of Chicago
- Dallas Museum of Art
- Solomon R. Guggenheim Museum, New York

NORMAN ROCKWELL

- Brooklyn Museum of Art
- Peabody Essex Museum, Salem, Massachusetts

UTAMARO AND JAPANESE PRINTS IN THE UKIYO-E STYLE

- M. H. de Young Memorial Museum, San Francisco
- Freer Gallery of Art, Smithsonian Institution, Washington, D.C.
- The Japan Ukiyo-e Museum, Matsumoto
- Los Angeles County Museum of Art
- The Metropolitan Museum of Art, New York
- Museum of Fine Arts, Boston
- Springfield Museum of Fine Art, Springfield, Massachusetts
- http://terminus. econ.rochester.edu/UKIYOE/index.html

DICK WEST

- Bacone College, Muskogee, Oklahoma
- Denver Art Museum
- Eastern Baptist College, St. David, Pennsylvania
- Thomas Gilcrease Institute of American History and Art, Tulsa, Oklahoma
- Heard Museum, Phoenix, Arizona
- Indian Center, Chicago
- Joslyn Art Museum, Omaha, Nebraska
- Museum of Northern Arizona, Katherine Harvey Collection, Flagstaff, Arizona
- National Gallery of Art, Washington, D.C.
- National Museum of the American Indian, Smithsonian Institution, New York
- Philbrook Museum of Art, Tulsa, Oklahoma
- Saint Augustine's Center, Chicago
- Seminole Public Library, Seminole, Oklahoma
- University of Oklahoma, Norman

CREDITS *(listed in order of appearance)*

Edouard Manet (1832–1883). *The Races at Longchamp,* 1866. Oil on canvas, $17\frac{1}{4} \times 33\frac{1}{4}$ in. (43.9×84.5 cm). The Art Institute of Chicago; Mr. and Mrs. Potter Palmer Collection (1922.424). Photograph © 1997 The Art Institute of Chicago. Robert Delaunay (1885–1941). *The Cardiff Team,* 1912–13.. Oil on canvas, $128\frac{1}{2} \times 87$ in. (326.4×221 cm). Musée d'Art Moderne de la Ville de Paris. Photograph © Photothèque Musées de la Ville de Paris. © L & M Services B.V. Amsterdam 980717. Myron (fl. c. 480–450 B.C.). *Diskobolos (The Discus Thrower),* c. 460–450 B.C. Roman marble copy of bronze original. Museo Nazionale Romano delle Terme, Rome. Photograph © Scala/Art Resource, New York. Jacob Lawrence (b. 1917). *Study for the Munich Olympic Games Poster,* 1971. Gouache on paper, $35\frac{1}{2} \times 27$ in. (90.2×68.6 cm). The Seattle Art Museum; Purchased with funds from P.O.N.C.H.O. Courtesy of the artist and the Francine Seders Gallery, Seattle. Photograph © Paul Macapia. Egyptian tomb painting. *Nofretari Playing Draughts,* c. 1290–1223 B.C. Copy of a wall painting from the Tomb of Nofretari (Valley of the Queens 66), $16\frac{7}{8} \times 18\frac{1}{8}$ in. (43×46 cm) (approximately 1:2 scale with original). Egyptian Expedition of The Metropolitan Museum of Art, New York; Rogers Fund, 1930 (30.4.145). Photograph © 1978 The Metropolitan Museum of Art, New York. Kitagawa Utamaro (1753–1806). *A Woman Watches Two Children Playing Blindman's Buff,* c. 1792. Polychrome woodblock print, $14\frac{1}{2} \times 9\frac{1}{2}$ in. (36.8×24.1 cm). The Metropolitan Museum of Art, New York; Gift of Estate of Samuel Isham, 1914 (JP 986). Photograph © 1994 The Metropolitan Museum of Art, New York. Dick West (1912–1966). *Cheyenne Winter Games,* 1951. Watercolor, $20 \times 26\frac{1}{2}$ in. (50.8×67.3 cm). The Philbrook Museum of Art, Tulsa, Oklahoma. Norman Rockwell (1894–1978). *Marbles Champion. The Saturday Evening Post* cover, September 2, 1939. Printed by permission of the Norman Rockwell Family Trust © 1939 The Norman Rockwell Family Trust. Jean-Baptiste-Siméon Chardin (1699–1779). *Soap Bubbles,* c. 1733–34. Oil on canvas, $36\frac{5}{8} \times 29\frac{3}{8}$ in. (93×74.6 cm). National Gallery of Art, Washington, D.C.; Gift of Mrs. John W. Simpson. Photograph ©1998 Board of Trustees, National Gallery of Art, Washington, D.C. Mary Cassatt (1844–1926). *Children Playing on the Beach,* 1884. Oil on canvas, $38\frac{3}{8} \times 29\frac{1}{4}$ in. (97.4×74.2 cm). National Gallery of Art, Washington, D.C.; Ailsa Mellon Bruce Collection. Photograph © 1998 Board of Trustees, National Gallery of Art, Washington, D.C. Alexander Calder (1898–1976). *Calder's Circus,* 1926–31. Mixed media: wire, wood, metal, cloth, yarn, paper, cardboard, leather, string, rubber-tubing, corks, buttons, rhinestones, pipe cleaners, and bottle caps, dimensions variable: $54 \times 94\frac{1}{4} \times 94\frac{1}{4}$ in. ($137.2 \times 239.4 \times 239.4$ cm) overall. Accessories: $76\frac{1}{2} \times 97\frac{3}{4} \times 96\frac{3}{4}$ in. ($194.3 \times 248.3 \times 245.7$ cm) overall. Pedestal box: $27 \times 76 \times 76$ in. ($68.6 \times 193 \times 193$ cm). Collection of Whitney Museum of American Art, New York; Purchase, with funds from a public fundraising campaign in May 1982. One half the funds were contributed by the Robert Wood Johnson Jr. Charitable Trust. Additional major donations were given by The Lauder Foundation; the Robert Lehman Foundation, Inc.; the Howard and Jean Lipman Foundation, Inc.; an anonymous donor; The T.M. Evans Foundation, Inc.; MacAndrews & Forbes Group, Incorporated; the DeWitt Wallace Fund, Inc.; Martin and Agneta Gruss; Anne Phillips; Mr. and Mrs. Laurance S. Rockefeller; the Simon Foundation, Inc.; Marylou Whitney; Bankers Trust Company; Mr. and Mrs. Kenneth N. Dayton; Joel and Anne Ehrenkranz; Irvin and Kenneth Feld; Flora Whitney Miller. More than 500 individuals from 26 states and abroad also contributed to the campaign (83.36.1-56). Photograph © 1998 Whitney Museum of American Art, New York. © 1998 Estate of Alexander Calder/Artists Rights Society (ARS), New York. Alexander Calder (1898–1976). *Cowboy on Horse from Calder's Circus,* 1926–31. Wire, wood, leather, cloth, cork, and string, $9\frac{1}{2} \times 24\frac{3}{4} \times 8\frac{1}{4}$ in. ($24.1 \times 62.9 \times 21$ cm). Collection of Whitney Museum of American Art, New York (83.36.19). Photograph © 1998 Whitney Museum of American Art, New York. © 1998 Estate of Alexander Calder/Artists Rights Society (ARS), New York. Jonathan Green (b. 1955). *Annette's Dolls,* 1990. Oil on canvas, 55×70 in. (139.7×177.8 cm). Jonathan Green, Naples, Florida. Maxfield Parrish (1870–1966). *The Reluctant Dragon,* 1900–1. Oil on board, $12 \times 8\frac{3}{4}$ in. (30.5×22.4 cm). Photo courtesy of the Archives of the American Illustrators Gallery, New York © Copyright 1998, ASaP of Holderness, NH, 03245 USA. Authorized by The Maxfield Parrish Family Trust. Pablo Picasso (1881–1973). *Paulo as Pierrot,* 1925. Oil on canvas, $51\frac{1}{4} \times 38\frac{1}{4}$ in. (130×97 cm). Musée Picasso, Paris. Photograph © Hubert Josse/Abbeville Press, New York. © 1998 Estate of Pablo Picasso/Artists Rights Society (ARS), New York. Marc Chagall (1887–1985). *The Magic Flute,* 1967. Color lithograph, $30 \times 21\frac{5}{8}$ in. (76.1×55 cm). Christie's Images, New York. © 1998 Artists Rights Society (ARS), New York/ADAGP, Paris. Winslow Homer (1836–1910). *The New Novel,* 1877. Watercolor, $9\frac{1}{2} \times 20\frac{1}{2}$ in. (24.1×52.1 cm). Museum of Fine Arts, Springfield, Massachusetts; Horace P. Wright Collection.